SNOW

GRANDEUR AND CALAMITY ON AN ARCTIC LANDSCAPE

GEESE

TEXT BY BRUCE BATT, PH.D.

Ducks Unlimited, Inc.

Memphis, Tennessee

1998

Author: Bruce Batt, Ph.D.
Editors: Chuck Petrie and Diane Jolie
Book Design: Dit Rutland

Published by Ducks Unlimited, Inc.

Gene Henry, President
John E. Walker, Chairman of the Board
Matthew B. Connolly, Jr., Executive Vice President
Chris Dorsey, Group Manager, Publishing and Communications
W. Alan Wentz, Ph.D., Group Manager of Conservation Programs

Cover photograph: ©Guy Fontaine
Back Cover photograph: ©Ty Smedes

ISBN 1-57223-182-3

Published April 1998

Printed in Canada

Library of Congress Cataloging-in-Publication Data

Batt, Bruce D. J.
   Snow geese : grandeur and calamity on an Arctic landscape / text by Bruce Batt.
      p.   cm.
   ISBN 1-57223-182-3 (pbk.)
   1. Snow goose--North America. 2. Snow goose--Migration--North America. 3. Bird populations--North America. 4. Endangered ecosystems--North America. I. Title.
   QL696.A52B38 1998   98-13037
   598.4'175'097--dc21   CIP

DUCKS UNLIMITED, INC.

The mission of Ducks Unlimited is to fulfill the annual life cycle needs of North American waterfowl by protecting, enhancing, restoring and managing important wetlands and associated uplands. Since its founding in 1937, DU has raised more than $1 billion, which has contributed to the conservation of over 8 million acres of prime wildlife habitat in all fifty states, each of the Canadian provinces, and in key areas of Mexico. In the U.S. alone, DU has helped to conserve over 1 million acres of waterfowl habitat. Some 900 species of wildlife live and flourish on DU projects, including many threatened and endangered species.

In memory of
Dale Doyle and Lindsay Gibson

Acknowledgments

Many individuals have provided facts, ideas, and opinions that I tried to capture in this book. Dave Ankney, Robert Rockwell, Ken Abraham, Robert Jefferies, Don Rusch, Ray Alisauskas, and Mike Johnson have become great colleagues and mentors on the ways of geese. Jim Leafloor really struck a spark on a Jet Ranger helicopter ride in June of 1996. Alex Dzubin, Graham Cooch, and Fred Cooke conducted or stimulated research on many of the issues covered in the following pages. Dave Ankney, Mike Johnson, Robert Rockwell, Mark Lindberg, and Scott Stephens provided critical review of early drafts of the manuscript, but I am responsible for interpreting what they told me.

I appreciate Matt Connolly's, Alan Wentz', Chris Dorsey's and Chuck Petrie's confidence in asking me to do this book. Editor Petrie was a tough taskmaster, but our friendship survived. Diane Jolie and Dit Rutland are outstanding professionals who rose cheerfully to impossible deadlines to make this team effort a reality. Brenda Carlson and Keith Ranier nicely handled myriad details and kept other things on track.

Finally, the Batt family was very tolerant as I responded to deadlines at the holiday season when more leisurely moments by the fireplace were called for. I thank them dearly for that.

TABLE OF CONTENTS

INTRODUCTION

In spring and summer, the tundra lowlands of coastal northern Canada erupt in pristine splendor. Rhododendron, purple saxifrage, and bearberry lend colorful accents to the lush, hummocky carpet of lichens and mosses that characterize the landscape. For almost nine months, locked in ice and snow and gripped by Arctic winds, subfreezing temperatures, and the interminable darkness of northern winters, the country appears silent and lifeless. But the lowlands begin to blush with life as the last spring snows recede. Then, as our planet progressively tilts its axis toward the center of its universe, the sun will illuminate the landscape longer each day, providing northern latitudes warmth and light for as much as 24 hours each day during the peak of the short, sun-saturated Arctic and subarctic summer.

It is this unrelenting, concentrated solar power that drives the coastal lowland ecosystem at high speed for about three months each year. The lowlands' diversity of habitat types—shallow ponds, low shrubs, and a narrow strip of coastal marshes—provides breeding grounds for a host of migratory birds that arrive there each spring. The amazing fecundity of the lowlands provides these birds and their offspring an implausible mass of invertebrate life and nutritious plants upon which to feed. Given the long hours of summer sunlight, the hatchlings can almost continuously attend to subsistence demands that require them to grow to near-adult size, fledge, and migrate south before September and the onset of winter.

The majority of birds nesting in the lowlands are waterfowl and shorebirds. Some are common; others are rarely seen in venues outside their breeding grounds. Tundra swans, northern pintail, American

©Arthur Morris

Oldsquaw ducks grace the tundra landscape throughout the Arctic in North America, Europe, and Siberia.

The coastal salt marsh provides habitat for a variety of bird species, including snow goose brood flocks.

The eerie calls of Arctic loons are commonly heard across the western Arctic landscape.

wigeon, oldsquaws, common eiders, Canada geese, and Arctic loons intersperse throughout this coastal habitat to nest as secluded pairs, seeking security in their isolation from competing pairs of their own species and from intrusions by predators such as Arctic foxes. Similar territorial and antipredator strategies are utilized by shorebirds such as Hudsonian godwits, golden plovers, stilt sandpipers, whimbrels, and common snipe, which also distribute their nests widely across the lowland habitat.

But another species of waterfowl that commonly breeds on the coastal lowlands adopts a different nesting strategy. The lesser snow goose is a communal nester. Adult breeding pairs congregate in nesting colonies where many pairs of eyes maintain vigil for encroachments by predators, and many voices can sound the alarm.

It is not this dissimilar antipredator strategy, however, that has caused populations of lesser snow geese, especially the Midcontinent Population, to grow to unprecedented numbers in recent years. These magnificent birds have lived in their natural environment for aeons, and their numbers have fluctuated in conformity with the biological economy afforded by their breeding, migratory, and wintering grounds.

But man-made alterations to the birds' habitat along their migratory paths and on their wintering grounds have caused their numbers to burgeon—numbers that their breeding grounds can ill afford. The fragile Arctic and subarctic areas where the birds assemble in spring

Hudsonian godwits migrate through Hudson and James bay in late summer on their way south to Tierra del Fuego.

and summer can no longer accommodate the masses of feeding snow geese that are stripping the tundra of vegetation faster than the plants, necessary to the well-being of geese and many other tundra-dwelling animals, can recover. The habitat damage is severe, and biologists acknowledge that an ecological catastrophe is unfolding—one that will affect not only snow geese, but all the other creatures that depend upon that same habitat for their very existence.

Few of us may ever see the tundra coastal lowlands of Canada, but many of us who appreciate migratory birds—although we may live thousands of miles away from their breeding grounds—will be affected by the ecological cataclysm brewing there. Helping people become aware of the impending disaster is important and will engender public support of wildlife managers' attempts to thwart it.

To that end, Ducks Unlimited, Inc. has undertaken the crucial task of bringing to the public a documentary movie filmed on the breeding grounds of midcontinent snow geese and along their migratory byways and wintering grounds. That movie and this book tell the story of the life cycle of these amazing "geese from beyond the north wind." Both, too, attempt to make all of us aware of what may become one of the most important wildlife crises of our time, and what we can do to meet its portentous challenge.

Matthew B. Connolly, Jr.
Executive Vice President,
Ducks Unlimited, Inc.

Ducks Unlimited's film crew observes the contrast between a patch of habitat protected from grazing and areas used heavily by feeding lesser snow geese.

Lesser snow geese and Ross' geese winter in the peaceful climes of the Bosque del Apache National Wildlife Refuge in New Mexico.

©Tom Vezo

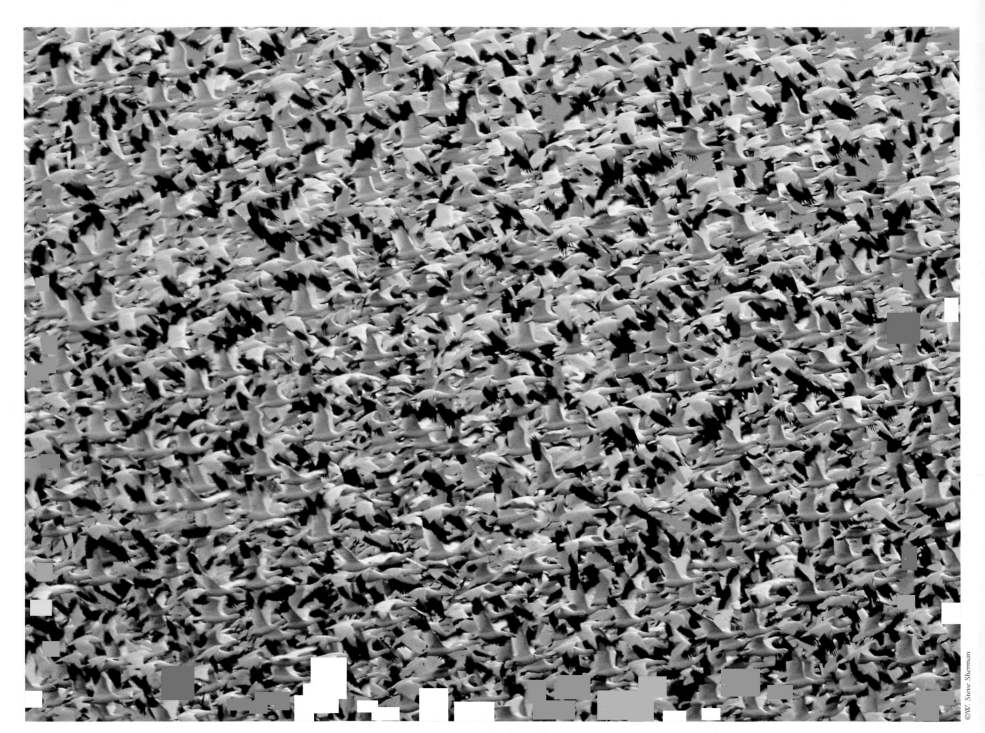

CHAPTER ONE

THE WHITE GEESE OF NORTH AMERICA

O "*Ooooh!* Wow! It looks like…like a snowdrift," remarked the 11-year-old through her shiny dental appliances.

"I bet my dad would like to be out there with his gun," declared the fifth grader with the Chicago Bulls hat stylishly placed backwards on his head.

"This is neat! Where do they come from? How many are there? Where are they going?" queried his nerdy, bespectacled chum.

"What a privilege, just to be able to see such a spectacle. We come every year. It's just marvelous!" explained the outgoing, van-driving mom who was supervising this ragamuffin gang from nearby Lincoln, Nebraska.

Fifty thousand snow geese were landing, sleeping, taking flight, feeding, arguing, swimming, preening, and standing guard while being stalked by a hungry coyote. They were also being watched by bald eagles in the nearby trees. All this was unfolding in front of the visitor's building at DeSoto Bend National Wildlife Refuge, just west of the town of Missouri Valley, Iowa, on the Missouri River.

The birds make this stopover every year in November and December while en route between their breeding and wintering areas. In some years, the geese have numbered more than 700,000 at DeSoto. Visitors average about 50,000 each year. Here and at many other sites in the U.S., Canada, and Mexico, people mark the change of the seasons by the passages of snow geese.

At Sachs Harbor on Banks Island in Canada's high western Arctic, the Inuit wait in May for the geese to return so they can harvest them and feast on the succulent, fat birds. Winter loosens its grip in that region for just a few weeks before the birds leave again with

©Bruce D.J. Batt

©John & Karen Hollingsworth

(*Top*) *The visitor center at the DeSoto National Wildlife Refuge provides superb opportunities for the public to observe migrant lesser snow geese.*

(*Above*) *As a bonus, visitors may sometimes witness the hunting tactics of coyotes.*

(*Left*) *Few scenes in nature are more exhilarating than that of a massive flock of snow geese during migration.*

1

A watchful eye is called for when bald eagles circle overhead.

©Ty Smedes

the new families they have raised during the short Arctic summer.

Near Nokomis, Saskatchewan, farmers dread the arrival of snow geese during the occasional wet Septembers when the harvest of wheat and barley crops is delayed. Not only do the geese love to eat these grains, which is a problem in itself for farmers, but the birds also trample and destroy more than they eat when it is wet.

In cornfields near Bombay Hook National Wildlife Refuge in Delaware, hunters spend many December days watching masses of snow geese fly by, out of range, en route to other fields where only other geese wait for them. But hunters keep trying because, on some days, the stars, the wind, the rain, and just plain luck line up to allow the waterfowlers to kill a few of the birds. Then, in a very real way, they enjoy the exhilaration of the harvest that human hunters have felt for centuries.

In the Nebraska Rainwater Basin, near Kearney, a couple of million snow geese stop in March and April each year as they head north. They concentrate in a few wetland areas with millions of other waterfowl that have also stopped, especially northern pintails, white-fronted geese, and sandhill cranes. Waterfowl managers worry that an outbreak of avian cholera in these dense concentrations of birds could cause hundreds of thousands of geese, ducks, and cranes to be converted to landfill or to be dumped onto goose funeral pyres. Snow geese carry cholera. Under the right circumstances the disease will kill them, and avian cholera is readily transmitted to other waterfowl, which are also susceptible to this hideous sickness.

So what are these snow geese? What do we know

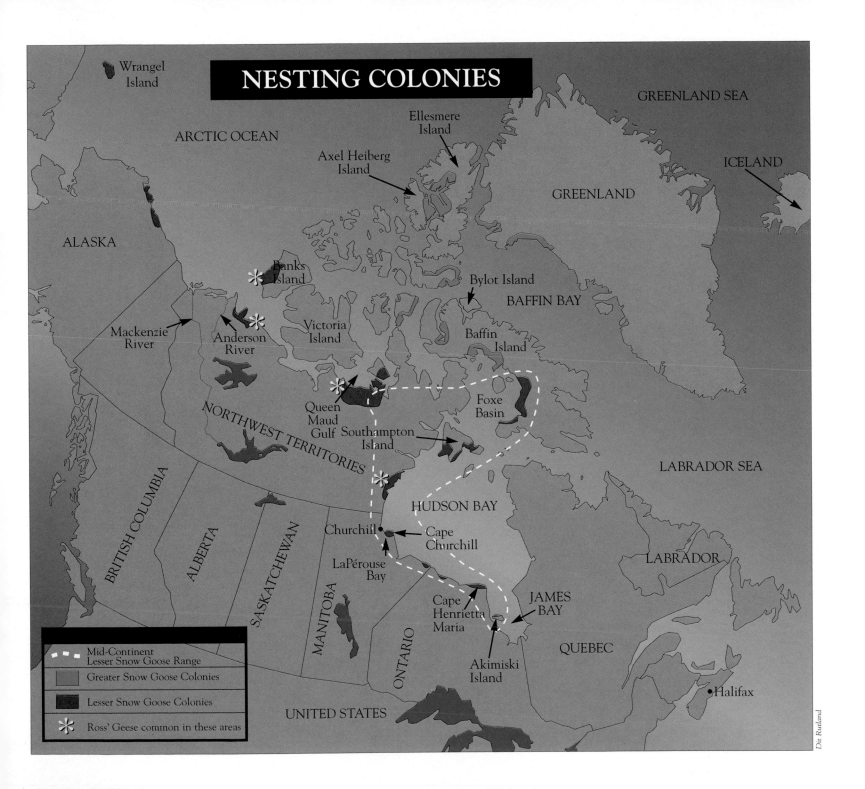

NESTING COLONIES

Wrangel
Island

ARCTIC OCEAN

Ellesmere
Island

GREENLAND SEA

Axel Heiberg
Island

GREENLAND

ICELAND

ALASKA

Banks
Island

Bylot Island

BAFFIN BAY

Mackenzie
River

Anderson
River

Victoria
Island

Baffin
Island

NORTHWEST TERRITORIES

Queen
Maud
Gulf
Southampton
Island

Foxe
Basin

LABRADOR SEA

BRITISH COLUMBIA

ALBERTA

SASKATCHEWAN

HUDSON BAY

Churchill

Cape
Churchill

LABRADOR

LaPérouse
Bay

MANITOBA

Cape
Henrietta
Maria

JAMES
BAY

ONTARIO

QUEBEC

Akimiski
Island

Halifax

UNITED STATES

Legend:
- - - Mid-Continent
Lesser Snow Goose Range

Greater Snow Goose Colonies

Lesser Snow Goose Colonies

✳ Ross' Geese common in these areas

Dit Rutland

3

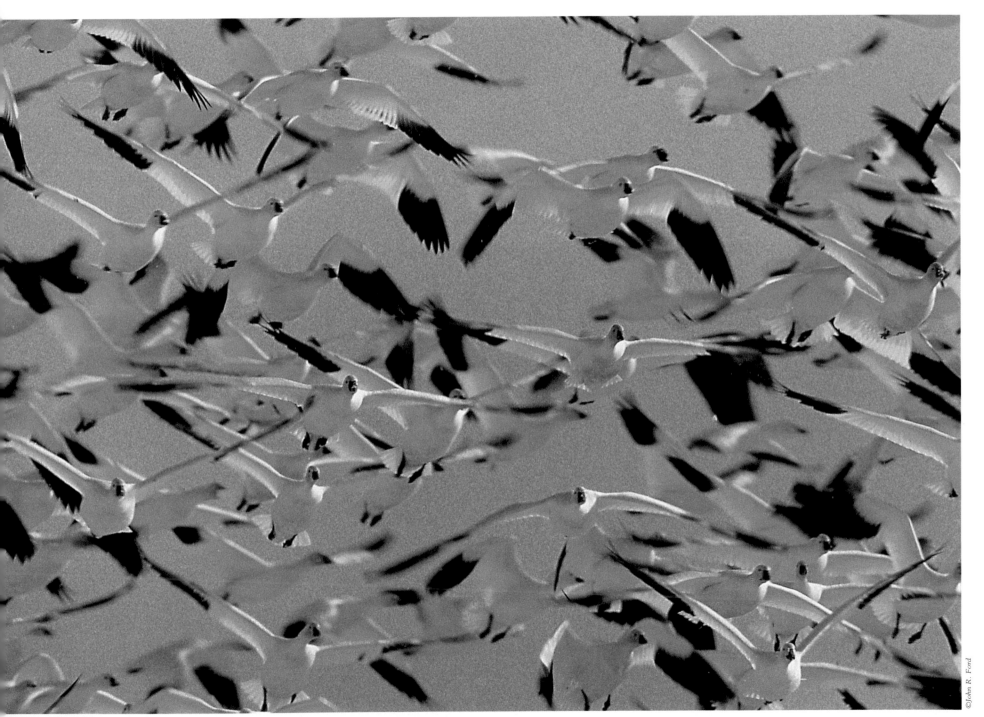

5

The Ross' goose (left) is smaller than the lesser snow goose (right) and has a different bill structure. The black color patch on the side of the lesser snow goose's bill is often called a "grinning patch."

©Gary Zahm

(Previous page) Ross' geese can create their own in-flight spectacles. The birds' short necks and the reddish-purple caruncles at the base of their bill distinguish them from the other white geese.

about them? Where do they live? Why are there so many of them? What's going to happen to them? Let's take a look.

In North America, there are three different kinds of "white geese": the Ross' goose, the greater snow goose, and the lesser snow goose. The three species breed in different locations in Canada's and Russia's Arctic and subarctic, and most winter in the U.S., although a few winter on the coast of British Columbia and some head for central Mexico.

This book will focus on just one of the populations of the lesser snow goose, but a look at the similarities, the differences, and the geography of all three white geese will help set the stage.

ROSS' GOOSE

The smallest of the white geese is the Ross' goose. Males weigh a maximum of 1,600 grams (3.5 pounds), females about 1,500 grams (3.3 pounds). Ross' goose population numbers have skyrocketed over the last 50 years. Fewer than 5,000 of the birds existed when their main nesting colony was discovered in 1940. More than 900,000 are alive today.

Ross' geese primarily nest in the Queen Maud Gulf area, but breeding pairs are also found on Banks Island and along the west coast of Hudson Bay. They nest in dense colonies, especially on islands that, due to their isolation, are protected from incursions by Arctic foxes. The increase in Ross' goose numbers in recent years has forced them to spread onto mainland nesting areas. Ross' geese are expanding to other new breeding areas too, and are difficult to distinguish from lesser snow geese during aerial surveys. In fact, the two species often occur in mixed colonies when nesting or in mixed flocks during migration.

The largest number of Ross' geese winter in the refuges and rice fields of the Central Valley of California. In recent years, they have also become abundant in New Mexico, especially at the Bosque del Apache National Wildlife Refuge in New Mexico, in Texas, and in north-central Mexico. Because of the rapidly expanding numbers of both Ross' and lesser snow geese, and their tendency to occur in mixed colonies, hybrids between the two species are fairly common.

The diminutive Ross' goose is one of the prettiest of the world's waterfowl. Its short bill is adapted to plucking stubby grasses and sedges. This may allow it to feed where bigger geese have consumed all the larger forms of grass. Its bill has distinctive caruncles, or warts, at its base. These become enlarged in older birds and are lacking in the young of the year. Bills are red and pale purple in adults. The legs of adult Ross' geese are pink; goslings' legs are yellow.

The Ross' goose's shrill, high-pitched call is distinctive

Greater snow geese look like larger versions of the lesser snow goose. All the white geese will take on orange feather staining, as seen on this goose, after feeding on roots and tubers where the soil has a high iron content.

and rather delicate in comparison to the calls of other geese. Its plumage is all white, except for black wing tips, which occur in all three species of white geese.

GREATER SNOW GOOSE

The greater snow goose is the biggest of the white geese. Adult males will weigh up to 3,600 grams (7.3 pounds). Females weigh about 3,000 grams (6.2 pounds)—double the size of the Ross' goose and 20 percent larger than the lesser snow goose. Greater snow geese number 600,000 today, but during the 1930s and 1940s there were likely fewer than 3,000.

Melanin, a pigment concentrated in the wing tips of white geese, produces the black coloration and increases the primary flight feathers' structural strength and resistance to wear.

©Arthur Morris

Like the Ross' goose, greater snow goose adults have an all-white plumage, as white as snow, except for the distinctive black wing tips. They have a black streak along the sides of their bill, which gives the appearance of a "grinning patch." The bill and legs are pink in adults, yellow to gray in the young of the year. Young birds have a distinctive gray plumage during most of their first year.

Greater snow geese nest farther north than the other white geese. Nesting colonies are found on the north end of the Foxe Basin on Baffin, Ellesmere, Bylot, and Axel Heiberg islands, and on northern Greenland. Musk oxen and snowy owls commonly share the areas where these snow geese nest. They winter along the Atlantic coast from New Jersey to North Carolina.

One of the greatest annual concentrations of greater snow geese occurs near Quebec City along the St. Lawrence River, where most of them stop during migration to stage in the spring and fall each year. The historic Cape Tourmente Club de Chasse managed the area for hunting until the 1970s, when it became the property of the Canadian government.

Along the St. Lawrence River, the geese feed heavily in the intertidal area, where they grub out the roots and tubers of grasses and sedges with their strong necks and bills. These areas are not big enough to feed all of the birds, so the geese have expanded their feeding activities up and down the river, where they exploit other marsh areas and farmlands. This results in conflicts with farmers whose pastures and crops are often damaged or destroyed by the geese, especially in the spring.

On the wintering marshes of the eastern seaboard, greater snow geese often eat out large tracts of coastal marshes by removing root masses of the vegetation there, leaving the marshes silt-laden, mucky, and of much reduced value for other wildlife. This feeding behavior is natural, but today's masses of greater snow geese destroy so much marsh that it does not recover as it once did during the summer growing season, when the birds are away breeding.

LESSER SNOW GOOSE

The male lesser snow goose weighs about 2,700 grams (5.9 pounds), the female 2,500 grams (5.5 pounds). Until 1961, it was thought that the lesser snow goose was closely related to another species, the blue goose, which associated closely with the lesser snow goose. We know now, however, that the lesser snow goose and the blue goose are actually the same species. Scientists call them the white and blue color phases of the lesser snow goose. Very few other birds show this trait, known as "plumage dimorphism." "Blues" and "snows," as they are commonly called, nest in mixed colonies and regularly pair and produce viable offspring.

The white-phase lesser snow goose has the identical all-white plumage and black wing tips displayed by other white geese. The legs and bill are pink in adults, gray and yellow in young birds. The grinning patch on the bill of both color phases of lesser snow geese is distinctive. Young white-phase geese are gray during their first fall. Young blue-phase birds have slate gray plumage all over, including the head. Blue-phase adults have a distinct white head and are sometimes called

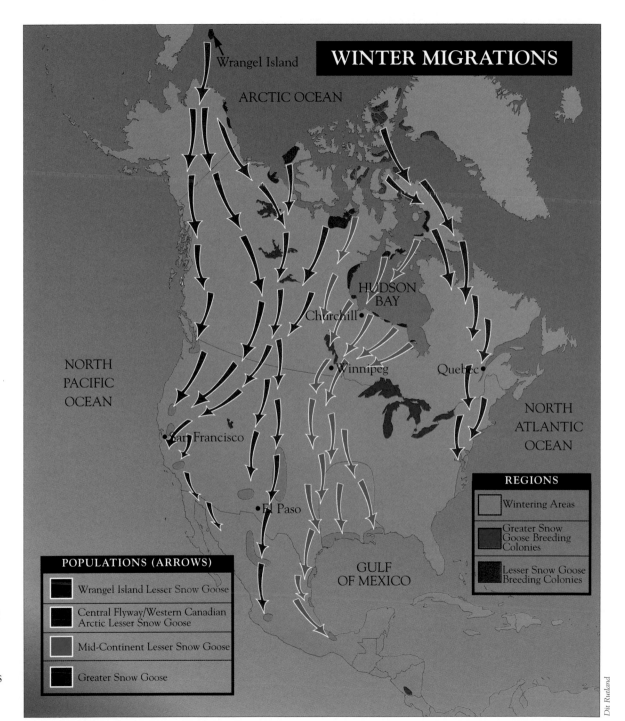

WINTER MIGRATIONS

Wrangel Island

ARCTIC OCEAN

HUDSON BAY

Churchill

NORTH PACIFIC OCEAN

Winnipeg

Quebec

NORTH ATLANTIC OCEAN

San Francisco

El Paso

GULF OF MEXICO

REGIONS

Wintering Areas

Greater Snow Goose Breeding Colonies

Lesser Snow Goose Breeding Colonies

POPULATIONS (ARROWS)

Wrangel Island Lesser Snow Goose

Central Flyway/Western Canadian Arctic Lesser Snow Goose

Mid-Continent Lesser Snow Goose

Greater Snow Goose

Dit Rutland

9

Snow geese exhibit both blue (left) and white color phases (center). In between exist a variety of blue-phase birds that show different portions of white feathers on the throat, breast, and rump (far right).

©Bill Marchel

"eagle heads." The rest of the body of a blue-phase adult has an intricate combination of gray, silver, cinnamon, white, and brown feathers that give an overall impression of a metallic-blue goose from a distance. Blue-phase birds make up about 80 percent of the lesser snow geese in eastern Arctic lesser snow geese breeding colonies. The proportion of blue- to white-phase individuals in breeding colonies decreases significantly as one moves west to northeast Siberia, where all the birds are white.

The lesser snow is likely the most abundant goose in the world, numbering at least 6 million during the last few years. There were probably fewer than 1 million as recently as 1950.

Waterfowl managers recognize four distinct populations of lesser snow geese: the Wrangel Island, the Western Canadian Arctic, the Western Central Flyway, and the Midcontinent populations. The most western of the lesser snow geese nest on Wrangel Island, off the north coast of Siberia, and winter on the coast of Washington, in British Columbia, and in Northern California. This population has declined from about 150,000 birds in 1970 to about 70,000 in recent years.

The Western Canadian Arctic Population nests on Banks Island, in the Anderson and Mackenzie river deltas, on Jenny Lind Island, and in the Western Canadian Arctic. It winters in central and southern California and in northern Mexico. These birds are abundant, but no counts of their numbers are conducted because they can't be distinguished from other populations with which they mix during the winter, when censuses are normally conducted.

The Western Central Flyway Population also nests on Banks Island and in the Queen Maud Gulf area. It winters in southeastern Colorado, New Mexico, the

©Mark J. Bilak

©Shannon Badzinski

(Top) After they molt and replace their old feathers each year, adult lesser snow geese are as white as snow, except for their black wing tips.

(Above) Blue-phase lesser snow geese are often referred to as "eagle heads."

©Bruce D.J. Batt

As soon as snow-free turf becomes available, geese descend upon it to feed by grubbing up roots and tubers. Lesser snow geese grubbed this coastal area near James Bay just minutes before the photo was taken.

three decades. These geese primarily nest around the southern and western shores of Hudson Bay and on Southampton and Baffin islands. They usually winter in Texas, Louisiana, Mississippi, Tennessee, Arkansas, and northeast Mexico. During warm winters, they may be found as far north as Missouri, Kansas, Iowa, and Nebraska.

TROUBLE ON THE TUNDRA

Most white goose populations have thrived during the last four or five decades, but waterfowl managers are deeply concerned about the future of these birds. Scientists and waterfowl managers believe there are too many white geese in some populations. When one thinks of the migration spectacles or the excitement of the kids at DeSoto, or when a hunter carefully smoothes the feathers of a beautiful specimen, the question, "How can there be too many of these beautiful creatures?" comes to mind.

The answer is that the masses of birds in some areas are destroying the very Arctic habitats upon which they and their young depend for sustenance. Many sci-

Texas Panhandle, and northern Mexico. Between 200,000 and 300,000 of these birds exist today. They overlap on the breeding grounds with the Western Canadian Arctic Population, but are more distinctive in their distribution during the winter.

The granddaddy of North America's lesser snow goose populations is the Midcontinent Population. About five million of these geese have concentrated on their breeding grounds in recent years. Their numbers have increased by about 5 percent per year for the last

At the end of the day, snow geese often roost on lakes and marshes where terrestrial predators, including man, are not a threat.

©Michael Frye

©Gary Kramer

entists believe that a point will be reached when the areas where white geese breed will not be able to sustain the birds any longer, and that their numbers will decline dramatically at some point in the future. How long it will then take for white geese and their breeding habitat to recover is not known, but it will likely require decades. Some biologists believe this will demand most of the next century, if such recoveries occur at all.

The numbers of midcontinent lesser snow geese and the damage these birds have already wrought on their breeding habitats are especially alarming. Ross' and greater snow goose numbers have also increased dramatically during the last couple of decades, but the damage to their habitats is less well understood.

The causes of the burgeoning white goose populations are believed to be several. Snow geese are extremely well equipped to thrive in the altered migratory and wintering ground landscapes on the Great Plains and Gulf Coast areas, where they live for about eight months of the year. They exploit waste agricultural grains and weeds that are in practically unlimited supply. The superb nutritional status of the birds contributes to high winter survival, and they usually arrive on their Arctic and subarctic nesting areas in good condition for breeding.

The birds' flocking behavior and their ability to avoid danger combine to make them an extremely wary and difficult game bird for hunters to harvest. The geese have also learned how to use private and public refuges most effectively, further contributing to the difficulty waterfowlers experience in harvesting them. Hunting is the main tool waterfowl managers utilize to build or to control most goose populations, but it is not very effective in managing snow geese. All these combined factors are driving the dramatic expansion of most white goose populations.

©Chuck Petrie

(Above) This lucky hunter has bagged a beautiful eagle head and a young white-phase lesser snow goose. Many hunting outings are much less successful.

(Left) A variety of agricultural crops provides a bounty of food for waterfowl. Alfalfa, where available and before it goes dormant for the winter, is a preferred staple of snow geese.

BEYOND TREE LINE

Tundra—the very thought of this haunting, alien landscape instills visions of polar bears, caribou, musk oxen, stifling swarms of mosquitoes and black flies, and spectacular vistas of pack ice, rocks, and spartan vegetation. It challenges the imagination: How did aboriginal people survive there? More than a life zone or a biological region defined by its flora, fauna, and native inhabitants, however, the tundra is one of the most compelling, wild frontiers on earth, especially for those who seek to experience life in a land where margins for error are slim—and life and death may be just seconds apart.

The glaciers of the Ice Age have been gone for several millennia, but, on the tundra, the scars they left are immediately visible. Here, there are places where it is possible to make a footprint or frame a photograph and be confident that no person may have ever come in contact with the same setting. The tundra is one of those environs, like desert mountains or pristine ocean shores, one seeks and savors just because it is there.

Plant and animal life on the tundra is defined by its short growing season, usually 60 days or less, and by prolonged periods of cold temperature. Trees are absent, unable to establish root masses in the layer of permanently frozen ground (permafrost) that reaches to only a few inches below the surface and that also eliminates niches for most burrowing mammals and all reptiles and amphibians. Dwarf spruce, willow, and birch plants survive in more southern and sheltered parts of the tundra, but they are absent farther north.

Arctic and subarctic temperatures on the tundra greatly restrict the rate at which plant material decomposes. Normally, less organic material decomposes each year than is produced by the growth during the short summer. Undecayed organic material thus accumulates

©John R. Ford

Stilt sandpiper pairs are often found on the same nesting territories in consecutive years. Their fall migration takes most of them to wintering grounds in South America.

(Left) The high Arctic tundra of Bylot Island provides strikingly beautiful breeding habitat for greater snow geese.

©Tom Vezo [c]

©Jack Hughes

(Above) The Arctic fox grows a thick, insulating coat that warms and conceals it during the long, frigid winter.

(Left) Cotton grass provides a cheerful and interesting highlight to the Arctic landscape.

as spongy peat saturated with water and also overlays bedrock and gravelly glacial deposits. The peat is usually covered with a living layer of lichens, grasses, sedges, and mosses. A modest variety of flowering plants have also adapted to the extreme environmental conditions of the tundra.

Animals that live on the tundra have taken two distinct evolutionary paths to cope with conditions there. One has been to develop physiological and behavioral characteristics that allow for survival throughout the year and reproduction when conditions allow. The Arctic hare, for example, has big feet that serve as snowshoes. Its fur provides superb insulation, and turns white in the winter to make it less visible to predators such as snowy owls and Arctic foxes. The hare uses terrain features, including resting on the leeward sides of snowdrifts, to find the most forgiving microclimates during periods of cold, windy weather.

Arctic foxes also turn white in winter. This helps conceal them as they stalk prey such as the hare. They grow an equally superb coat of new fur each year, immediately prior to the onset of winter. They raise their young in the summer, taking advantage of the expansive food resources, especially waterfowl, their eggs, and their young, which are then available to predators. Foxes cache some of this abundance of summer to be dug up and eaten when it is needed later, in winter, when they also seek out lemmings, ptarmigan, and Arctic hares. Many Arctic foxes also move onto

Polar bears are forced ashore along the Arctic coast when the sea ice melts, but they return to the ocean as soon as it freezes to spend the winter hunting seals.

©Richard Mousel

19

Along Hudson Bay, snow geese are already nesting by the time the ice pack has broken up and moved off shore.

21

Unlike the coloration and parental behaviors of most other birds, the red-necked phalarope female is the more brightly colored of the two sexes; the less-colorful male incubates the pair's eggs and raises their young.

©Tom Vezo

the sea ice, where they follow polar bears and clean up the food scraps the bears leave behind, usually remnants of marine mammals such as seals.

Other residents of the tundra exhibit similar adaptive characteristics that allow them year-round occupancy in its harsh environment. Each new generation of mosquitoes and black flies lies dormant most of the year as eggs and larvae, ready to hatch and proliferate as soon as the thermal stopwatch gives the go-ahead signal. In winter, lemmings live in networks of tunnels under the snow where, at a depth of one foot, the temperature may be 50 degrees Fahrenheit higher than it is one foot above the surface. Musk oxen grow one of the most remarkable fur coats in all of nature, and simply carry on feeding and performing other life functions on the open tundra all winter. Polar bears head out onto the ice pack, where they hunt seals. The bears are such good hunters that they come to the shore in summer, at their peak annual body weight, to wait for the ice to form again.

The other main evolutionary path has been simply to avoid the harsh majority of the Arctic year by migrating to other places where the temperatures, at least, are more benign. Spectacular assemblages of migratory birds seasonally visit the tundra each year. The masses of waterfowl and shorebirds are, by far, the most striking and noticeable species, but some gulls, shrub- and ground-nesting sparrows and warblers, and raptors thrive under similar itinerant lifestyles. To facilitate the short breeding season on the tundra, another adaptation of migrant animals such as geese and other northern-nesting birds is that their young grow faster and fledge sooner than do those of their southern-nesting relatives, since tundra-hatched goslings and chicks can feed almost continuously during the long hours of summer sunlight.

Summer provides long days and the warmth that drives an explosion of life in the Arctic. Yet every living plant or animal there has only weeks to blossom, set seed, lay eggs, hatch, grow, shed old feathers or fur, or grow new antlers, as well as put on body reserves for winter. Summer's profusion of life on the tundra is indeed a biological phenomenon, but that abundance is restricted to a very narrow window of opportunity.

THE COASTAL SALT MARSH: WHERE THE TUNDRA MEETS THE SEA

Where the elevation gradient is gradual and other environmental factors are favorable, the transition zone between ocean and land is occupied by a unique ecosystem: the salt marsh. In more temperate climates, salt marshes are dominated by cordgrasses, reeds, and spikerushes, which often grow chin high to a man and higher. Near the equator, these coastal areas are dominated by mangrove swamp forests. Complex communities of other plants, birds, mammals, amphibians, and reptiles live in these ecosystems, which often serve as nurseries for many shellfish, finfish, and invertebrates that spend their adult lives in the sea. Salt marshes are routinely described as the most productive ecosystems in the world.

In northern latitudes, large portions of the thousands of miles of island and mainland coastline of the tundra are also occupied by salt marshes. These marshes are discontinuous—absent where the coasts are rocky, are steeply sloping, or are still occupied by remnant glaciers. However, Arctic and subarctic salt marshes have become established where coastal areas possess the appropriate gradual changes in elevation, favorable temperatures, and tidal amplitudes that allow their formation.

In North America, the coastal salt marsh of the Arctic has been most comprehensively studied along the Hudson and James Bay coasts, from the Quebec-Ontario border to the Northwest Territories (NWT) immediately north of the Manitoba-NWT border, a distance of about 1,200 miles. The surface geology of this coastal ecosystem is inextricably linked to the last continental glacier, the Wisconsin Glacier, which completely covered this region of North America some 10,000 years ago.

Every aspect of the Hudson and James Bay coastal region has been influenced, in some way, by this glacier and its subsequent retreat. The lowlands are underlain by glacial deposits, and the changes in elevation there are very gradual. Several miles offshore of the west coast of Hudson Bay, for example, it is not uncommon for a person in a kayak to run aground on rocks deposited by the glaciers and subsequently moved around by the bay's pack ice.

(Right) Where the terrain is flat, the coastal salt marsh is expansive. In other areas it will only occupy a narrow strip of coastline or will be absent altogether.

(Below) Willow ptarmigan are one of the few nonmigratory bird species that live in the Arctic year-round.

©Tom Vezo

A feature not apparent to the casual observer is that the land here is emerging from the ocean at about the rate of one centimeter per year. This phenomenon is caused by the expansion of marine soils and sediments that were compressed under the crushing mass of the glacier. The technical term for this rebounding is "isostatic uplift."

Farther inland, where the topography is better drained and more terrestrial, the land is rising at the same rate. Like the marine muds along the coast, the soil under these inland areas also contains a complement of oceanic salt. Typical of this inland habitat, where organic soils have accumulated for many decades, the vegetation is dominated by lichens, mosses, and stunted woody plants. The surface is also more hummocky, because of frost heaves. The tops of the hummocks can be very dry, even though they remain frozen just a few inches below the surface. These inland areas are caribou and ptarmigan habitat, but even these animals remain concentrated along streams and ponds, where there is a greater diversity of vegetation. Isolated pairs of Canada geese may nest in freshwater ponds far-

ther inland, but the vegetation around these interior wetlands is inadequate to support many geese.

Between the newly emerging land at the edge of the bay and the more terrestrial and less saline area farther inland lies the salt marsh. It is occasionally swept by high tides and is typically wet, but only occasionally holds standing water. The marsh is, structurally, a very simple ecosystem dominated by two species of plants with pretty-sounding but tongue-twisting names. One is a sedge (*Carex subspathacea*) and one is a grass (*Puccinellia phryganoides*). Both grow very low to the ground, reaching just a few inches in height.

These plants are foods that are highly preferred by geese, which typically crop them very close to the ground, often giving the salt marsh the appearance of a manicured lawn. The geese and these plants have become nicely adapted to each other: The plants provide excellent nutrition for the adult geese and their young, and then respond to the grazing by proliferating shoots and rhizomes that actually increase the amount of new green vegetation the geese can feed upon. Grasses and sedges all over the world have made simi-

©Stuart Slattery

Canada geese are solitary nesters throughout the Arctic.

(Left) Two adult lesser snow geese rest with their two drab-plumed young and an adopted blue goose gosling.

(Right) Young geese of all species are led by their parents to feeding areas soon after hatching.

(Far right) This lush, green goose pasture on Bylot Island has been heavily used by greater snow geese, as evidenced by the vegetation's close manicure, the scattered feathers, and goose droppings.

lar adjustments through evolutionary time, whether they've been grazed by geese, buffalo, field mice, dairy cows, or lawn mowers.

In the Hudson Bay lowlands, the prime feeding area for snow goose broods is the coastal salt marsh. Indeed, research has shown that where grasses and sedges have been lost, goslings grow less vigorously and are forced to move elsewhere to feed. Otherwise, they will experience lower growth and survival rates. As a result of a critical loss of their preferred food sources, in fact, an increasing number of goslings are starving to death.

Arctic-nesting geese return to the tundra in early to mid-May

RETURN TO THE TUNDRA

Snow geese arrive on the Hudson Bay marshes in mid-May. Three or 4 million of them will concentrate on the lowlands and wait for temperatures to warm and snow to melt so they can begin nesting in early June. Only about a million of these geese nest on the lowlands, however; the rest move farther north to nest in huge colonies at places like Southampton and Baffin islands.

The geese arrive paired. Pairing among adult males and females is thought to last for as long as both adults are alive, but widows and widowers will take a new mate if the other is lost. "Divorce" among snow geese is considered rare, but scientists have observed formerly paired birds, identified by colored leg bands, with new mates in subsequent breeding seasons.

Surviving offspring from the previous breeding season likely arrive back on the colony with their parents and siblings, but afterward become independent and strike out on their own. Up until then, the young birds' parents have led them everywhere, and family cohesiveness was crucial to their survival. Now they return to familiar territory, because individual adult female geese usually nest near the same site each year. The gander, whether he is the goose's same mate from the previous year or not, likely will have originally come from a different colony. New pairs form during the winter, when large flocks from different colonies join together, and, to a female snow goose, the geographic location of the male's colony seems to have no bearing on his acceptability as a mate.

The female chooses a mate from the many white- and blue-phase suitors that are available to her in winter. What traits does she assess when sorting through the potential choices of mates? Scientists have only

Yearling geese and non-breeding adults assemble on or near the breeding grounds in "bachelor flocks" after the breeding adults have started nesting.

©Chuck Petrie

Snow goose pairs seek relative isolation even in the largest nesting colonies.

©Michael Frye

concluded that she is likely to choose a mate that is the same color as her parents. Thus a goose with two white-phase parents will likely pick a white-phase mate. One with blue-phase parents may be white or blue herself, but she will more likely pick a blue-phase mate because her parents were blue.

Nesting must begin by early June in order for the young to grow and be ready to migrate south by early September, at the latest. It takes a week for a female snow goose to lay eggs, another three and one-half weeks to hatch them, an additional six to seven weeks for the young to grow and learn to fly, and a bit longer to gain the strength necessary for migration. By then, it's late August, and winter is just a week or two away.

Spring weather is the variable that most affects the success of a breeding season. If conditions stay cold and the ground remains snow covered until mid-June, many birds won't nest. Some may lay smaller clutches of eggs and raise some young, but the net effect is that the fall flight—the total number of adults and young migrating south after the breeding season—will be much smaller following late springs. For a bird that can

*te-phase snow
look like little
ow fuzz balls.*

©Arthur Morris

live for two decades or more, it is smart to skip breeding during years when the chances of successfully raising young are low. Besides the physical demands nesting requires of the female, sometimes actually leading to her starvation near the end of incubation, nesting is also risky because of the greater exposure to predators she faces while on her nest.

Female snow geese incubate their eggs almost non-stop for about 24 days. Very little time is taken away from the nest to feed, because ravens, parasitic jaegers, herring gulls, and Arctic foxes are quick to zero in on unattended nests. Even caribou and polar bears have been observed taking snow goose eggs. Furthermore, the mandate to complete breeding within a narrow

time frame requires near-constant incubati[on]... bation period is extended when the goose [leaves the] nest, which causes the temperature of her [eggs to drop].

While the goose is incubating, the gand[er] alert for danger, but he is able to feed and [gain] weight. Later, after her eggs hatch, the fe[male] feed nearly full-time, while the gander m[aintains] vigilance over her and the goslings.

Goslings are not fed by their parents. [Within] a few hours after hatching, when the y[oung dry] off and look like little fuzz balls, the pa[rents lead] to feeding areas, usually near the nest [site. The] goslings instinctively begin to feed the[mselves, peck]ing at vegetation.

Canada goose and whi[te]
goose goslings [have]
yell[ow...]

Communication between family members starts even before the eggs hatch and continues throughout the first year of life, after which the young become independent of their parents

(Right) Preparing for a spring subsistence hunt, Cree Indians make blue goose decoys by setting out lumps of dirt adorned with white Styrofoam heads.

©*John R. Ford*

During the brood-rearing period, both parents molt most of their old feathers, including the wing feathers, which allow flight. The adults are then grounded for about three weeks and regain flight at about the same time their goslings are ready to take their first aerial steps.

Throughout brood rearing, the parents and young vocally communicate. Indeed, while still on her nest, the female utters soft murmurs and grunts, increasing her vocalizations as hatching time approaches. The young evidently take all this in, as they respond to the vocalizing female immediately after they hatch. They produce low-volume peeps at first, which mature into gravelly, adolescent *wa wa wa, wa wa wa* sounds and into the familiar high-pitched calls of adult snow geese, all within a year.

SPRING ARRIVAL AND SALT MARSH DESTRUCTION

With such narrow time restraints controlling their reproductive success, it is crucial that the geese arrive on their breeding areas in the best physical condition possible and be ready to breed as soon as temperature

conditions allow. The birds are at their peak weight and physical condition in May, immediately prior to nesting. At this time, they weigh about 50 percent more than they did on their southern wintering grounds in January. (That fact accounts for the premium that Cree and Inuit hunters in some northern communities place on harvesting a good supply of snow geese each spring.)

The birds' superior body condition means they are virtually not dependent upon food supplies on the breeding areas just before nesting. In effect, they bring their own "groceries" with them from their migration layovers on the northern Great Plains of the U.S. and Canada. Most female geese have enough nutrients stored in their bodies to finish the last stages of migration, lay their eggs, and incubate nearly continuously for more than three weeks.

Nevertheless, energy reserves must be preciously conserved, and the geese take every opportunity to feed before they begin nesting. On the Hudson Bay lowlands, the birds feed voraciously on salt marsh vegetation and in freshwater areas away from the coast as

37

©Tanya Handa

Windrows of plant debris are left behind where grubbing snow geese have nipped off the succulent parts and discarded the remainder of the plants.

(Right) Grubbing is serious business, and hard work.

©Arthur Morris

soon as they return to the North. As the tundra snows melt, patches of the previous year's vegetation slowly become exposed. The geese descend on these areas as they become available. The birds use their heavy, serrated bills to grub out the plants' roots and tubers, which are where all the grasses' and sedges' nutrients have been stored since the previous September. They also pull up dead and newly growing stems, which have nutritious tissue living at their bases. The geese clip off these stems and discard the rest of the plant.

These feeding methods are remarkably effective in helping the birds maintain and sometimes even improve their body condition, and they've been nourishing themselves like this for millions of years. Although the birds' feeding methods are very destructive to the plants, scientists believe the geese historically existed in low enough numbers that the vegetation could generally recover from one spring to the next.

Scientists also believe that this formerly somewhat stable plant-herbivore equilibrium has been thrown out of kilter during the last half of the 20th century. Today there are so many snow geese returning to some Arctic

and subarctic breeding grounds each year that the plants no longer have time to recover between the annual feeding onslaughts of migrant geese. In fact, vast areas of the Hudson Bay lowlands are rapidly being converted to nearly bare soil that is dry and cracked in the summer, and is becoming very saline. Evaporative drying of the soil transports salts from underlying sediments to the surface, where the salts are left behind, in some places at more than three times their concentration in seawater.

The resulting high salinity makes it impossible for most sedges and grasses to survive, and a new community of salt-tolerant plants unpalatable to geese has become established. Eventually, though, even these plants succumb and only bare, saline soil remains. Adult geese can feed on a wider variety of plants than can goslings, so upon their return to the lowlands in spring, the adults move inland to fresher wetland and upland habitats to find food. Their destructive feeding

©Shannon Badzinski

Recent grubbing (foreground) is surrounded by pools of water that have inundated areas that snow geese grubbed during previous years.

methods are exercised there too, and soon the grasses, sedges, and other plants have been grubbed and pulled out, and the expanding wave of destruction moves both inland and up and down the coast.

On freshwater areas farther inland, salt is also a problem, as it rises to the surface when the soil dries out and erodes. As a result, native willow bushes and other shrubs die, and freshwater ponds become saline and can no longer support their typical plant and animal communities.

At breeding colonies away from the lowlands, the critical feeding habitats are usually farther inland and are not close to salt marshes. Nevertheless, every major lesser snow goose colony is showing signs of ecosystem damage, and scientists agree that the wave of Arctic ecosystem destruction caused by burgeoning snow goose populations is expanding year after year.

Quantifying the destruction in these remote areas is expensive and difficult. Scientists have estimated that 35 percent of the total salt marsh habitat along the 1,200 miles of Hudson Bay coastline from the Ontario-Quebec border to the Manitoba-Northwest Territories border has been destroyed. Another 35 percent has been severely damaged. At the most-studied snow goose colony, at La Pérouse Bay, Manitoba, more than 90 percent of the salt marsh has been destroyed, and additional habitat damage is evident several miles inland.

Climate cycles also likely contribute to the degradation of the salt marsh along the Hudson Bay and James Bay lowlands. During the last few decades, there have been a series of years during which May and June temperatures over northern Hudson Bay and Baffin Island have been two or three degrees below normal. These late springs detain millions of migrating snow geese destined for the huge colonies on Baffin and Southampton islands for up to two weeks longer than usual on the lowlands. This is the very time of year when the birds' destructive feeding is most prevalent. Thus, cold springs contribute heavily to the destruction of the lowland salt marshes, as well as to areas farther inland.

DEATH ON THE TUNDRA

On the Hudson Bay lowlands, the most important feeding areas for snow goose young are the coastal salt

A skeleton is all that remains of a willow bush that succumbed to increased soil salinity after geese stripped the grasses and sedges from the land around it.

©Shel Zolkewich

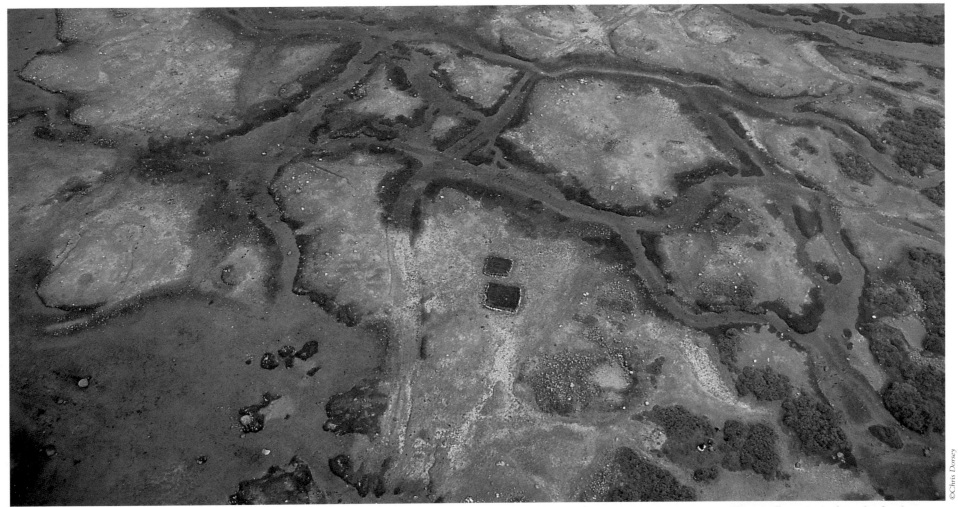

©Chris Dorsey

Two small green patches of sedge (center foreground) have been protected from geese by a fenced exclosure on this devastated landscape. Green plants along the waterways are species that tolerate high salinity, but they are not eaten by goslings.

marshes. The plants there provide the optimum mix of nutrients for healthy growth, which will take the goslings from 100-gram hatchlings to 1,700-gram fledglings less than two months later. On other colonies away from the Hudson Bay lowlands, goslings depend on some of the same plants, but also have a few additional species that provide their nutritional requirements.

By hatching time, tundra plants have sprung to life, driven by the sun's warmth and paced by their own short window of opportunity to propagate. Just as things get going for the plants, however, the goslings hatch and are immediately grazing on the tender new

41

43

stems and shoots. Thus, the grazing pressure on the salt marshes is continuous throughout the ice-free period.

Snow geese parents lead their young from the nest site to feeding areas along the coastline. On a healthy salt marsh, this may be only a few yards away. Most goslings will first learn to fly within a couple of miles from their nest site. However, as the wave of salt marsh destruction by geese expands each year, the parents must lead their young farther and farther away from the nest site to find adequate food. Scientists have commonly observed goslings—their toe webs marked with tiny metal tags while still in the nest—more than 25 miles from their nest sites when they were trapped for banding six weeks later.

These energetically expensive overland movements result in lower gosling growth rates and, ultimately, smaller adult body sizes. Some adults choose to try to raise their young near nest sites where gosling food is inadequate. These goslings grow even more slowly and suffer high mortality. By early August, one can go to the most damaged nesting colonies, such as the one at La Pérouse Bay in Manitoba or the colony at Cape

Henrietta Maria in Ontario, and readily find goslings immobilized by starvation and kidney failure. Lack of freshwater in what is becoming a very saline environment contributes to these kidney problems, but the final agent of death is often a parasitic infection that produces a disease known as renal coccidiosis. It is common, too, to see orphaned goslings—those left behind, not strong enough to keep up with their parents as they led the rest of their brood to better feeding areas.

Even though some people would comment that this is Mother Nature's way, the scenes of dead and dying goslings are extremely disheartening to witness—and they are being repeated tens of thousands of times each year on the most damaged colonies.

The destruction around snow goose brood-rearing areas is expanding annually. The movement of broods outward from traditional colony nesting areas is one cause of the widening destruction. A second cause is the young female's instinct to return to the area from

©Bruce D.J. Batt

On the most degraded colonies, malnourished, orphaned goslings are common, as are carcasses of other goslings that have succumbed to starvation, disease or predation.

(Left) Snow goose families have been forced to move away from their nesting colonies into areas used by brood-rearing Canada geese. The habitat shown here exhibits bare patches and other signs of degradation from overuse by geese.

45

Healthy freshwater tundra wetlands (above) present a stark contrast to the devastated habitat of this ravaged salt marsh near Cape Henrietta Maria.

which she herself fledged, to establish her own nest site when old enough to breed. Because most of the young geese that live to fledge have been moved a long way from where they hatched, the effect is to expand the geographical boundaries of the colony's nesting area.

Dr. Robert Rockwell of the American Museum of Natural History has more than 25 years' experience studying snow geese at La Pérouse Bay. He compares the destruction of snow goose breeding colony habitats to the human problem of urban blight and sprawl: As the cores of many of our cities become crime ridden and the quality of life there plummets, the next generation moves out to the suburbs, where a happier family life is possible. As the cities' degraded cores continue to expand, however, many of the subsequent generation will move even farther away, into more-distant suburbs. But if neighboring cities' boundaries eventually grow together, there will be no place left to move.

There is a finite amount of habitat into which snow goose colonies can expand. On the Hudson and James Bay lowlands (1,200 miles of coastline), there are almost no areas remaining that have not been destroyed, degraded, or at least heavily grazed by the geese. At some other colonies the damage is apparently less advanced, but it is conspicuous and heading down the same path as the destruction occurring in places like Cape Henrietta Maria and La Pérouse Bay.

The time is near when there will no longer be areas into which the lowland snow geese can expand. All the brood-rearing habitat will have been destroyed. Gosling survival will move below the level needed to sustain the population. At that point the population will decline as the birds die from old age and other natural mortality factors. It is reasonable to think of this as a population "crash," but it will likely take place over a couple of decades and not precipitously, like the periodic population nosedives experienced by snowshoe hares, lemmings, and ruffed grouse.

In the process, however, tens of millions of goslings will starve to death.

CANARIES OF THE SALT MARSH

The coastal areas used by snow geese are also used by a wide array of other migratory bird species. Ecosystem degradation by snow geese affects them too. Some of these birds nest on the salt marsh, others use it as feeding habitat while nesting elsewhere, and some just stop over en route to their nesting or wintering areas farther north, south, east, or west.

Some data exists by which we can measure the changes in how these other birds utilize the coastal lowland areas. Most of the information comes from the La Pérouse Bay study area, where some striking changes have been recorded.

At least one species has all but disappeared. The yellow rail once *tap-tap-tapped* the researchers to sleep each summer night. They are no longer heard at the research camp. Several shorebirds have become significantly less abundant at La Pérouse too, including short-billed dowitchers, Hudsonian godwits, whimbrels, semipalmated sandpipers, red-necked phalaropes, and stilt sandpipers. Among the waterfowl, American wigeon, oldsquaws, northern shovelers, and red-breasted mergansers were once common, but are now rarely found. Apparently, the drying out and salinization of the freshwater wetlands and streams have decimated

©Tom Vezo

the plant and animal food supplies upon which these birds depended.

At Cape Churchill, less than 20 miles east of the La Pérouse Bay snow goose colony, biologists have studied the nesting of Canada geese for almost three decades. The Canadas that nest there belong to what is known as the Eastern Prairie Population. The researchers at Cape Churchill rarely observed snow goose broods when their work started there in 1970, when there were fewer than 2,000 snow goose pairs at La Pérouse Bay. Throughout the 1990s, however, the biologists observed snow geese in the area all summer long, and

©John & Karen Hollingsworth

(Top) Whimbrels nest in marshes along Hudson Bay as well as in the high western Canadian Arctic, northern Europe, and Siberia. They have declined markedly at La Pérouse Bay, however, as the snow goose colony there has expanded.

(Above) Yellow rails are no longer heard at night at the La Pérouse Bay research camp.

47

some now nest there. A few days after the 40,000 or so snow goose nests hatch at La Pérouse Bay, the Canada goose study area is literally overwhelmed with snow goose families moving down the coast in search of food. Many of the Canada goose brood-rearing areas on the Cape Churchill study area have now been turned into bare, saline mudflats, and few Canada geese now nest on the Cape.

A related phenomenon has apparently occurred on Akimiski Island in James Bay, where the nesting Canada geese of the Southern James Bay Population have declined dramatically over the past two decades. The cause is degradation of the Canadas' preferred salt marsh brood-rearing habitats. Snow geese are the culprits here, too. Only a few pairs nested on Akimiski Island in the 1970s; more than 2,000 pairs nest there today.

The extensive destruction of Akimiski's salt marsh is thought to have occurred during the 1980s when cold springs held a few hundred thousand snow geese back from their migrations to colonies farther north, again at just the time of year when the birds are feeding so voraciously before nesting. At Akimiski, the degrada-

(Below) Parasitic jaegers remain abundant at La Pérouse Bay, where they are opportunistic nest predators.

(Below right) The North American population of northern shovelers is at very high levels, but this duck has disappeared as a nester from La Pérouse Bay, where freshwater ponds are now too saline to produce the shoveler's preferred foods.

©Arthur Morris

©Cathy & Gordon Illg

The La Pérouse Bay research camp (background) now sits in an expansive landscape of devastated habitat that formerly supported a thriving population of lesser snow geese.

©Diana Pollak

51

©Jonathan Thompson

©Jonathan Thompson

Malnutrition has seriously affected feather development in this Akimiski Island Canada goose gosling (bottom photo), in comparison to that more typically seen on a gosling (top photo) of the same age that found good pasture on which to feed.

(Right) Biologists mark some geese with plastic neck collars to provide information on the birds' migratory pathways, wintering sites, and annual survival.

(Previous page) In August, researchers round up brood flocks of snow geese for banding.

tion appears to be further aggravated by nonbreeding Canada geese from southern Canada and the northern U.S. that spend the summer there. All this pressure on the limited habitat has led to low gosling survival among the local nesting Canada geese.

Of the waterfowl and shorebirds affected by snow goose habitat destruction, no continental populations have been seriously threatened. Indeed, the northern shoveler population—one of the species affected by snow goose intrusions on their habitat—is more abundant at the end of the 20th century than it has been since shovelers were first surveyed in 1955. The birds, nonetheless, are like the canaries taken by miners into coal mines: When the canaries stopped singing, there was something seriously wrong with the environment of the mine. And the fact that shovelers, stilt sandpipers, and yellow rails don't breed at La Pérouse Bay anymore indicates that something is seriously wrong with the salt marsh.

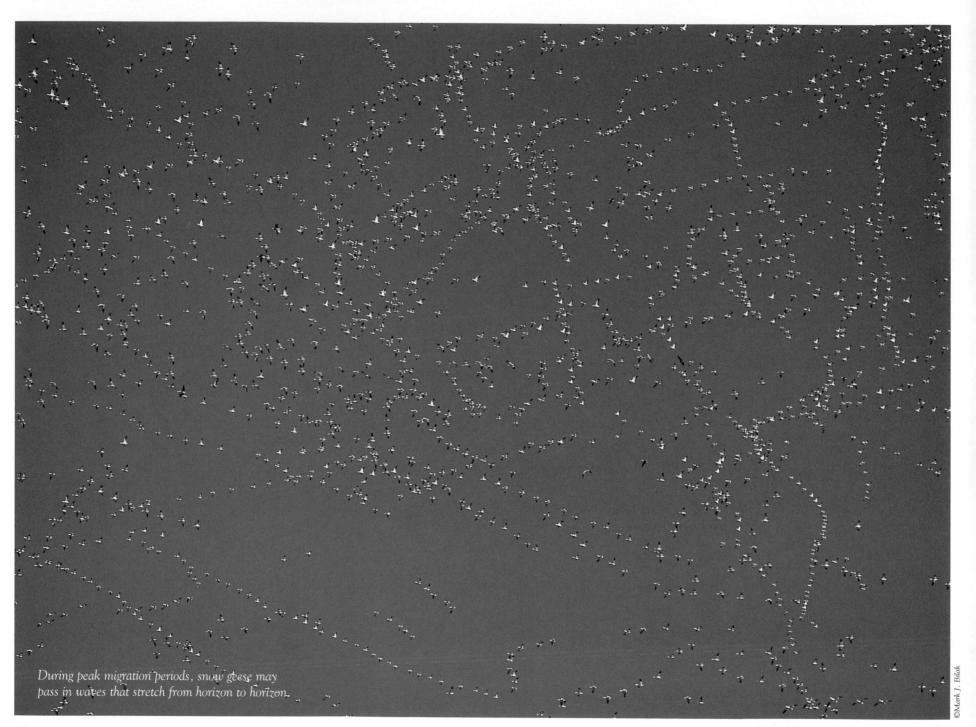

During peak migration periods, snow geese may pass in waves that stretch from horizon to horizon.

©*Mark J. Bilak*

OUT OF THE ARCTIC

W"Wavies" is what John Boreskie called snow geese when they flew over southern Manitoba in the spring and fall. They came in waves from horizon to horizon.

"Hmmm," I thought. "That's kind of corny." But John was my dad's friend, so I didn't say anything.

As a kid with a curious attraction to waterfowl, I listened to everything Mr. Boreskie said about ducks and geese, and I believed most of it. He was the first mentor to share his books and his understanding of waterfowl, including snow geese, with me.

Most intriguing was where the snow geese came from— "the Arctic"—and where they were going—"to the States somewhere." The former scientific name for the snow goose, *Chen hyperborea*, had it about right—"goose from beyond the north wind." And when they migrate north or south, as opposed to local

movements between feeding areas and roosting sites, they do come in waves. Wavies is a good name too.

ONTO THE GREAT PLAINS

In early August, snow geese leave their breeding areas and head south. They've done their best to fatten up on the stems, seeds, and berries of grasses, sedges, and other plants. Blueberries are a favorite—a preference shared with bears. At the end of August, near Churchill, Manitoba, local snow geese concentrate near the airport to feed on blueberries that grow on the same esker on which the runways are built. The birds loaf on the asphalt approach road, which turns bright purple for a few weeks in September. (The pigment that makes the berries blue isn't affected by digestion as it passes through a snow goose.)

©Lon E. Lauber

©Bill Marchel

(Top) Blueberries are a favorite late summer food on drier inland habitats.

(Above) By mid-September, adult geese and their new families arrive on the prairies and begin an eight-month period during which they consume large quantities of agricultural foods.

An adult blue-phase snow goose and a young white-phase bird descend on a harvested cornfield.

©Jason Saucier Jr.

It takes time for young birds to determine what is food and what is not.

©Arthur Morris

These geese from the Hudson Bay lowlands have a long southern journey ahead of them; the geese that breed on Baffin Island, another 700 to 800 miles north, face an even longer journey. They all have to cross the vast boreal forest of northern Canada before they can put down on the farmlands of southern Canada and the northern U.S. At least that's what they do now, at the end of the 20th century. In the first half of this century, many snow geese flew nonstop to the coastal marshes of Texas and Louisiana, and were only occasional fall visitors to the farmlands in between. A few snow geese still arrive at the mouth of the Mississippi River or on the Brazoria National Wildlife Refuge in Texas by early October, but these represent only a tiny fraction of the birds that stop farther north.

Why the geese now stop in such massive numbers on the prairies isn't fully understood. Snow geese hardly ever stopped in southern Manitoba in 1960, when I first learned to call them wavies. Now, a million or more may stop there every year, and biologists don't know why.

At least three explanations for the change seem plausible. First, the expansion of agriculture all the way to north-central Manitoba and Saskatchewan has presented the geese with an enormous food supply that wasn't there before settlement. Because they are creatures of habit and are well adapted to living in marshes, it probably took a few decades for the birds to start using these and other farmlands.

Dennis Raveling, one of the most introspective goose biologists of this century, believed that once geese learned from their parents where to go and what to eat, and they survived those experiences, they would likely repeat them every year for the rest of their lives. During migrations subsequent to their first southern journey in fall, and their return trip to the breeding grounds in spring, in which they are led by their parents, however, young birds are more likely to try new things. These include exploring and occupying new habitat, a process called "pioneering." It is likely that young snow geese were the first of their race to pioneer the farmlands. Plenty of good food and high survival meant that those were safe places to bring their own

While favoring farm fields, snow geese explore many places in search of edible foods, including the roots, tubers, and seeds of wild plants.

families when they were old enough to breed.

As snow goose populations have grown and their breeding habitat has deteriorated, young birds may also have been forced to migrate south before they were fit enough to fly all the way to the Gulf Coast. Those families may have had to stop short of their traditional wintering grounds and tarry where they found plenty of food, which allowed them to stock up for the rest of the trip south. Again, those same young birds were likely the ones that started leading their own young to those new safe places a few years later. Snow goose family structure, with the attendant geography and feeding area lessons, has a lot to do with why geese go where they go.

Heavy hunting pressure in more southern areas may also have caused birds to move around in search of safer places to spend the winter. Most of these would have been north of their traditional wintering sites in Gulf Coast wetlands. Those young birds that spent their first

While the largest numbers of snow geese migrate through the midcontinent region, many winter farther west at places such as Bosque del Apache Refuge in New Mexico, where they may share feeding areas with sandhill cranes.

©Arthur Morris

Bosque del Apache National Wildlife Refuge has all the attributes that make up desirable wintering habitat, including a good food supply and safe roosting areas.

winters farther north in safer places likely also brought their own families there in subsequent years.

Waterfowl managers have increased the availability of safe places for geese farther north. They have created safe places on refuges, and even whole states and provinces that only allow half-day hunting, to keep the birds from moving farther south. In Texas and Louisiana, public agencies and private citizens maintain refuge roosting ponds to make sure the birds aren't scared off by hunting pressure.

The snow goose's uncanny ability to exploit these safe places and to avoid hunters are important factors contributing to its high survival rates and growing populations. Waterfowl managers believe this will become increasingly relevant as time goes on and the number of experienced older birds in snow goose populations increases.

EXPLOITING THE FARMLANDS

By mid-September in a normal northern prairie fall, farm crops have been harvested, and there is plenty of spilled grain left behind in the fields. Waste wheat and

Two adult blue-phase adults may have lost their young to predators, hunters or starvation.

©Guy C. Fontaine

barley have become traditional staples in the diets of geese and ducks, but corn, field peas, lentils, and even alfalfa are now also heavily used by migrant waterfowl. In the midcontinent states, corn is the main crop residue exploited by the birds; soybeans are used to a lesser extent. In the main wintering areas in the South, rice is used heavily, as is milo. In all these areas, the birds also consume various types of weed seeds.

During years of abundant fall precipitation, farmers in Manitoba, Saskatchewan, and the Dakotas experience considerable problems when snow geese join mallard

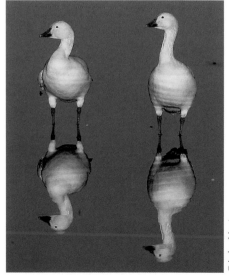

A white-phase adult pair, "sitting pretty."

©Arthur Morris

ducks and Canada geese to feed in crops that have yet to be harvested. Besides eating a great deal of ripened grain, the birds destroy even more by stomping swathed wheat and barley into the mud. When conditions in fall are dry, harvest and field work proceed on schedule, and the geese merely take advantage of crop residues.

Elsewhere on migratory stopover points and during the winter, until about the end of December, snow geese are not considered a problem for farmers. In fact, many farmers enjoy having them around, as they believe the geese help them by consuming weed seeds that would otherwise have to be dealt with in the spring with herbicides. Southern rice farmers with "red rice" weed problems are particularly glad to see the birds.

From the end of January until snow geese leave on their northern migration, however, farmers in states like Arkansas, Kansas, and Nebraska do have problems with snow geese in their winter wheat fields. By then,

(Right) Grain silos are everyday features of snow goose habitat after the birds leave the Arctic.

(Far right) Across prairie Canada and the northern United States, snow geese feed voraciously in harvested wheat, barley, lentil, and pea fields during September and October

©Bill Marchel

©Rodney Schlecht

©Chuck Petrie

much of the spilled grain has been cleaned up or has rotted or sprouted, and new crops of winter wheat are just beginning to grow. Now, as the days get longer and the birds are beginning to feed more heavily to store away reserves for migration and nesting, farmers in those states have to be constantly vigilant. Thirty thousand to 50,000 snow geese can do extensive damage if they settle on a 60-acre winter wheat field. Losses can easily be 80 percent, or more, of the crop— a potential $20,000 loss to the farmer.

It is this ability of the geese to live and thrive on the agricultural landscape for up to eight months of the year that has perhaps contributed more than anything else to the booming Midcontinent Lesser Snow Goose Population. In fact, most species of wild geese are admirably equipped to take advantage of agriculture on the Great Plains, and most goose populations of all species are thriving. This is in stark contrast to the status of many grassland birds that live on the Great Plains but need native prairie to be successful.

Sometimes the birds find fall-seeded grain crops, such as winter wheat, where they are not welcome.

Because of their inability to adapt to environmental changes, prairie-adapted bird populations have declined much more than those of most other native North American birds. Some animals just can't make it on farmlands, which is why species such as greater prairie chicken, bobolink, and upland sandpiper are becoming increasingly rare. On the other hand, species including geese, white-tailed deer, and blackbirds are thriving in the agricultural landscapes that have been laid out for them.

WINTER HOMES

The traditional wintering area of the Midcontinent Lesser Snow Goose Population is the coastal marshes of Texas and Louisiana. Thousands of birds still winter there, but the largest portion of the population now winters on farmland as far north as Tennessee, Missouri, Oklahoma, Kansas, and north Texas. Some of the largest concentrations stop in north Louisiana and Arkansas, areas that attracted very few snow geese 30 or 40 years ago.

This movement from the Gulf Coast to the farmlands

Few species of wildlife are as gregarious or vocal as snow geese.

was facilitated by a multitude of factors. One was certainly the expansion of the rice industry, and agriculture in general, following World War II. With this increased agricultural production, foods that had never been in such abundance before were soon available to the birds.

For instance, rice growing has expanded enormously in the South in the last four decades, and it is a common management practice for landowners there to

65

As the sun rises, geese awaken and start calling and moving about, apparently anticipating their coordinated, outbound movements to farm fields for feeding.

In wetland-poor California, lesser snow geese and other waterfowl are restricted to roosting on state and federal refuges, where they rest between jaunts to food-laden agricultural fields.a

flood harvested rice fields. Most species of waterfowl and many other species of waterbirds benefit from this management practice. There are several other environmental benefits. For one, fields covered with water undergo much-reduced wind and water erosion, improving air and water quality. Flooded rice stubble decomposes during the winter, saving the farmer fuel and time in the spring when he prepares the land for planting. Finally, the birds also eat spilled grain and weed seeds, which saves herbicide expense.

Another reason why snow geese largely abandoned their traditional coastal wintering grounds was likely the degradation of the marshes there when substantial amounts of freshwater were cut off from the coastal plain by a vast network of irrigation ditches. Loss of the freshwater inflow, coupled with the expansion of the Intercoastal Waterway and oil exploration channels, resulted in saltwater intrusion, which greatly diminished the quality of the coastal marshes.

The snow geese that still winter on Gulf Coast marshes are natural and crucial components of the coastal ecosystem. These geese exploit their natural marsh food supply by using their strong, serrated bills to grub out the nutritious roots, rhizomes, and tubers of plants that grow in intertidal areas. In the process, the geese open up solid stands of cordgrasses, cane, and sedges, exposing the soil and creating open water areas. These open areas provide habitat niches for other birds that would not be there if the geese had not done their part first. The presence of snow geese in the coastal marsh creates winter habitat for species such as greater and lesser yellowlegs, least sandpipers, willet, marbled godwits, dowitchers, black-necked stilts, phalaropes, pectoral sandpipers, marsh hens, coots, egrets, bitterns, and a variety of ducks and other geese. Because of this increase in the diversity of species and the number of individuals that can benefit from the marsh's resources during the winter and the rest of the year, ecologists label animals like the lesser snow goose a "keystone

Long-billed dowitchers and many other shorebirds use tracts of Texas Gulf Coast marshes where snow geese have grubbed out openings in dense stands of grasses and sedges.

species," for the snow goose's very presence affects the structure and diversity of the whole ecosystem.

NORTHWARD IN SPRING

Snow geese start moving north from their wintering grounds by early February. Some of their most spectacular gatherings occur at this time of year as they push

Destructive feeding by snow geese in Gulf Coast marshes creates habitat in areas that would otherwise not be available to many types of waterbirds.

©Ryan Galatti

Spring migration is a rather leisurely affair. The geese press against the snow line as it recedes northward from March until May.

against the retreating snow line. When they reach Nebraska and Iowa at the end of the month, they exploit the remaining spilled agricultural crops that have been preserved under the snow since the previous fall. Modern reduced tillage practices help assure that the waste grain is not buried. Cold temperatures keep it

from sprouting.

In spring, the birds feed more heavily than at any other time of the year, and they are constantly moving from field to field in search of sustenance. During the three months of spring migration, they consume enormous quantities of food, which allows them to migrate, maintain themselves during frequent weather reversals, and increase their weight by 25 percent.

One of the most spectacular spring concentrations of waterfowl, including hundreds of thousands of lesser snow geese, occurs in the Rainwater Basin of Nebraska. Pintails, white-fronted geese, sandhill cranes, and myriad other waterfowl move through this continental waterfowl funnel each year. In the early 1980s, about 10,000 snow geese staged there. In the late 1990s, there are often more than a million. The Basin has become one of those safe places, at least for now, that snow geese exploit so well.

However, wildlife managers believe a disaster is in the making in the Rainwater Basin. Disease outbreaks that have killed a few tens of thousands of birds have occurred there before. Burgeoning numbers of avian-cholera-carrying snow geese pose an ominous potential for devastation.

In the spring, snow geese do not concentrate on many of the same areas they used in the fall. Also, snowmelt temporarily floods many formerly drained and seasonal wetlands across a wide front as the snow line retreats, providing the geese many places to rest.

The last prairie stopping places for the geese are on the northern boundaries of agricultural activity in Manitoba and Saskatchewan. However, many birds likely take the last big steps back across the boreal forest to the Hudson and James Bay lowlands from farther south. The geese arrive on the lowlands, in waves, about mid-May, to await warmer weather so that breeding can begin. The entire coastline is used by the geese to some extent, but their most significant concentrations are found on James Bay just south of Cape Henrietta Maria, and at a few other places along Hudson Bay in Ontario and Manitoba.

Snowmelt and the exposure of tussocks of grass in early June will signal the beginning of a new year's nesting effort and the production of another crop of young snow geese. Thus the cycle begins anew.

©Bill Marchel

©F. Eugene Hester

(Top) Throughout spring migration, the geese remain intimately linked to agricultural food subsidies.

(Above) Food and safe roosting sites are the key elements of snow goose habitat during spring migration.

71

In spring, snow geese are busy feeding, courting, and migrating. The end of the day, however, as darkness sets in, is usually a quiet, restful period.

©Michael Frye

CHAPTER FIVE

A LOOK TO THE FUTURE

Most species of geese found in North America are extremely well adapted to thrive in the environment that our modern civilization has helped create. Exceptions are a few species or populations that have special problems, such as the dusky Canada goose, whose nesting area in Alaska was destroyed by an earthquake, or the Atlantic Flyway Canada goose, which was once overharvested. Others are species such as the emperor goose and the Atlantic and Pacific populations of brant, which are stable in number or are below long-term population averages. None of these three latter geese use agricultural crops for food, as each still lives in the native habitat to which it adapted over thousands of years of evolution. These geese have not benefited from the nutritional subsidies provided by modern landscapes and are at population levels that are more sustainable by their breeding ground habitats.

The problem of overabundant lesser snow geese poses some unprecedented challenges for natural resource managers. In many areas of the world, goose populations are generally higher than they have ever been in history.

In North America, greater snow and Ross' geese are at unprecedentedly high numbers. In fact, they have each proportionately increased to a greater extent than has the Midcontinent Lesser Snow Goose Population. There are serious conflicts between the greater snow goose and the agricultural community around St. Lawrence River spring staging areas, and coastal marsh habitats also suffer extensive overgrazing on the birds' wintering areas on the East Coast of the U.S. Reduced gosling

Snow geese in a banding trap anticipate their immediate future, which is safe in the hands of a biologist. Their long-term future, though, is clouded with ominous uncertainty.

An adult snow goose joins a mass of other geese during spring migration near Mitchell, South Dakota.

By spring, this 10-month-old blue-phase snow goose is beginning to look like its parents.

(Far right) Spectacles like this one, on a southern Manitoba landscape in spring, beg the question, "How can there be too many of these beautiful creatures?"

growth rates and adult body sizes are occurring in Ross' geese and greater snow geese, as witnessed in devastated lesser snow goose colonies. Damage on the Arctic breeding grounds used by Ross' geese and greater snow geese is also under way, although it hasn't been as extensively studied and documented as it has been on lesser snow goose breeding colonies.

FUTURE GOOSE (ARCTIC ECOSYSTEM) MANAGEMENT

Society has many choices to make on goose management issues. For those populations that remain at problematically low levels, management interventions that may be most helpful in increasing them are unlikely to be very controversial. Reducing hunting mortality, establishing new wildlife refuges, and instituting predator management are traditional tools that can be utilized either to reduce mortality or to increase the production of young in those populations.

In theory, at least, managing overabundant geese is actually not all that different. The causes of overabundance all relate to increased survival and breeding suc-cess. Many populations of geese are managed quite precisely by increasing or decreasing the allowable hunter harvest. For most species, particularly the so-called "dark geese" (Canadas, white-fronted geese, and the two populations of brant), populations can be maintained essentially at target levels by setting specified harvest goals in the respective states and provinces.

In North America, the same practices of varying allowable hunter harvest have been tried by waterfowl managers to reduce white goose populations to levels that are more sustainable on their available breeding habitat. However, the snow goose's extraordinary adaptability to agriculture and its ability to elude hunting mortality have allowed it to "escape" traditional management restraints, and its numbers are growing out of control. The limited availability of Gulf Coast marsh habitat, which formerly restricted the species' numbers, has effectively been removed as a population control factor. Instead, nutritional subsidies have assured that the geese will arrive on their breeding colonies in superb condition almost every year, regardless of the poor condition of those habitats.

Few scenes in nature are more memorable than encounters with snow geese coming to their evening roost.

©Tom Vezo

©Chuck Perrie

©Michael Hill

(Top) The abundance of most geese can be managed by varying the allowable hunter harvest to build or reduce bird numbers. These measures, however, have had little impact on most snow goose populations over the last decade.

(Above) Greater snow geese, like these wintering birds feeding on a farm field in Delaware, are also at record high population levels.

Population biologists have concluded that adult survival is the most important factor driving the size of most goose populations. Snow geese live an average of about eight years and normally breed about six of those years. After they have survived their first year, more than 80 percent survive each subsequent year. That means that if each adult pair produces even two broods during those six breeding years, the population will continue to grow. As a result, anything that might be done to reduce their reproductive success would have

to be done every year across a huge area to reduce the population. Little can be done on the breeding grounds in the way of habitat management, however, and nothing practical can really be done to reduce the production of young.

Reducing adult survival is the only realistic way to control goose populations. Controlling hunting mortality is how we now modify adult survival, and additional methods such as poisoning the birds or rounding them up for slaughter are other possibilities. These latter methods are socially unacceptable, however, so more effort and higher success rates by hunters seem to be the paths to most vigorously pursue.

Future management of problem goose populations will have to consider allowing hunters some of the old tools that were taken away from them when there was a need to increase waterfowl populations—techniques like baiting and the use of electronic calls. Other new opportunities to harvest the birds must be considered. A migratory bird treaty between Canada and the U.S. forbade spring hunting and market hunting because those practices were deemed to cause excessive harvest

80   SNOW GEESE

and a decline of migratory waterfowl numbers. But these practices may be just what we need to reinstate, at least for a while.

This report will leave those debates to scientists and wildlife managers, and to professional resource agencies and the conservation community. Here, I can only offer a fervent call to action to get on with the job and decide how to reduce snow goose numbers to a level that can be sustained for the foreseeable future—and then do it.

Failing to act will allow degradation to continue until habitats used by the geese and other species will be lost for decades, perhaps for most of the next century, and maybe forever.

During that time, tens of millions of goslings will starve to death, which in itself is a dreadful enough final thought for this story. The problem of snow goose overabundance is one we have clearly identified. We caused it, and we can anticipate a coming ecological catastrophe. There's still time to solve the snow goose problem—if we act immediately and decisively. The lessons learned in reconciling this dilemna will be cru-

©Arthur Morris

cial, as other goose populations may be heading down the same path.

To allow our man-made problems to reduce the presence of the snow goose to that of a rare visitor, to lose the spectacles of migrating and staging birds, and to allow the continued destruction of a portion of the Arctic that supports a whole community of wildlife will not be acceptable to those who follow us. We owe more to those kids at DeSoto, and to ourselves and our grandchildren.

(Above) This pair of snow geese arrived in Louisiana in November with only one gosling. Many pairs arrive with no young of the year at all, as their offspring are unable to grow and mature to flight stage on the degraded habitats of their breeding colonies.

(Left) Scenes like this will become rare if snow goose numbers are not reduced to levels that can be sustained by their Arctic breeding grounds.